WATER THE EARTH

WATER THE EARTH

A STUDENT'S GUIDE TO MISSIONS

AARON LITTLE

CF4•K

10 9 8 7 6 5 4 3 2 1
© Copyright 2014 Aaron Little
ISBN: 978-1-78191-321-5

Published in 2014
by
Christian Focus Publications,
Geanies House, Fearn, Tain,
Ross-shire, IV20 1TW, U.K.

Cover design by Paul Lewis
Printed and bound by Bell and Bain, Glasgow

MIX
Paper from
responsible sources
FSC® C007785

CONTENTS

INTRODUCTION: INCREDIBLE INDIA

India has to be one of the most fascinating places on the planet. It's home to all of the world's major religions, to endless wonders both ancient and modern, and to 1.2 billion people speaking some 400 different languages. Its history is almost as old as history itself, and the richness of color and culture is simply without compare.

Planting my two American feet on Indian soil was a lot like being born, like seeing the world for the first time. My travels to Europe, South America, and eastern Asia were no primer for India. This was a world all its own.

The familiar grays and blues of American and European fashion seemed bland compared to the rainbow assortment of Indian silks and saris. Cows, monkeys, and small livestock roamed freely on even the main thoroughfares as hordes of people clamored to bumpers and open windows of already overcrowded city buses, some even taking passage on the roof! Buses dodged taxis, taxis dodged rickshaws, rickshaws dodged motorbikes, and motorbikes dodged bicycles. The all-too-clever street vendors seemed to fill in the gaps with their feeding frenzy on the color-clad pedestrians, and especially on the white-skinned, backpack carrying, water-bottle drinking tourists like me.

It was these bustling byways of Delhi and Agra that brought me face to face with some of the world's most awesome wonders like the Taj Mahal and Agra Fort. Yet in India, as I would learn quickly, awesome wonders are overshadowed by tragic diseases. The Indian spirit of hope hangs in the balance between the grandeur of cultural celebration and the sobering reality of affliction—poverty, prejudice, and prostitution—just to name a few.

I can remember waiting at the entrance to the Taj Mahal—that great, enchanting pillar of Indian achievement. Tourists from the world's richest nations stood shoulder to shoulder with India's "untouchable" Dalit beggars, the poorest of the poor. Worlds collided here, and I was standing at the center of it.

Up until this point, my only concern had been my fullest enjoyment. There had been no rhyme or reason to my Indian adventure, only that I be entertained every step of the way. Yet somehow, my worldly bliss was being replaced by a heavenly consciousness. My folly was beginning to be my shame, and my shame was giving way to resolution.

I pictured myself as some kind of Robin Hood, stealing from the rich to feed the poor, as if redistributing the world's wealth would solve the issue of poverty.

Or perhaps, like Jean Valjean (Les Misérables), I might vindicate the oppressed, rescuing prostitutes from street corners and caring for their orphans. Could that be the answer for this troubled land?

I thought of India's most pre-eminent advocate of peace and independence, the beloved Mahatma Gandhi, who did so much to bring justice and equality to his people. But would abolishing the age-old caste system really solve the problem of prejudice?

I took a seat at the north end of the Taj Mahal estate overlooking the Yamuna River and peered out over the thick walls and iron fences. I fixed my eyes on a large funeral pyre where, with great fanfare, Hindu priests were offering last rites for the dead. I thought of the man who lay there, whose life had now expired. What sort of man might this have been and for what purpose had he been born? What legacy had he left behind? And as his body now burned away, what of his soul?

My thoughts turned inward as I pondered my own life. My dying heart continued to beat, but for what purpose and for how long? My heartbeats were numbered, and each one brought me closer to the last. The sights and smells of India filled my curious body today, but tomorrow this would be just a memory, that is, if tomorrow ever came. I opened my eyes a little wider, trying to take everything in, but holding onto a moment is like holding the wind. It's always slipping away. And for our man on the funeral pyre, all was gone already—and forever. He would join another 80,000 that day who would die without knowing the good news of salvation through Jesus Christ.

Yet here I was, rescued and redeemed. I had been ransomed from the grave and the funeral pyre, and my destination was secure in Christ. No power on earth or below the earth could stay me from the resurrection power of the Cross. The only problem was the disconnect somewhere between my heart and my hands.

That disconnect, however, was not in some kind of inability or unwillingness to serve. On the contrary, I was able and willing. My problem lay much deeper than that. I had an *identity* problem, and it had all but cut off my senses.

But as I breathed deep the smoke from funeral pyres and fresh cooked curries, as I witnessed slums and sacred splendors, as I gorged myself on the spices and specialities of Indian cuisine, as I wrestled with stories of both hope and affliction, and as I allowed myself to cry and to laugh with real people in real time, something changed. Despite all the life and activity that surrounded me, I became all too keenly aware of a vast emptiness—even deadness—and it completely revolutionized my perspective on missions.

You see, to take a journey toward a fresh understanding of missions, we have to understand where it begins and ends—and I found that it's really in the same place. It's not in stealing from the rich to give to the poor. It's not in abolishing prejudice or rescuing orphans and prostitutes, not even in planting churches—but in *worship.*

PART 1:
A THEOLOGY OF MISSIONS

CREATED TO WORSHIP

"Worship, therefore, is the fuel and goal of missions." – John Piper

Why Do I Live?

Yohannan was the youngest of six boys, born into poverty in the village of Niranam in southern India. He would not wear shoes until after his seventeenth birthday, and even then, his ninety-pound frame hardly filled them. Yet God had a mysterious plan for this humble village boy.

At age eight, God brought young "Yohannan" salvation, and at age sixteen, God called him to missionary service in northern India. For the next seven years, this young man tirelessly labored in bringing the gospel to all he encountered, many of them having never even heard the name of Jesus.

Eventually, through the miracle of God's sovereignty, this young man would be led to the persons and the means by which he would come to study the Bible in the US—and the rest would quickly become history.

Today, K. P. Yohannan is founder and president of the largest mission organization in the world, *Gospel for Asia*. He has published hundreds of books and stirred countless people around the globe toward a fresh understanding of missions. In his various writings, he often relays stories and conversations from his Indian missionary journeys. In one particular account from *Revolution in World Missions,* K.P. describes a friendly exchange he had with a young Indian student there.

"What are you doing?" I asked the lad.

"I go to school," was the reply.

"Why do you go to school?"

"To study," he said.

"Why do you study?"

"To get smart."

"Why do you want to get smart?"

"So I can get a good job."

"Why do you want to get a good job?"

"So I can make lots of money."

"Why do you want to make lots of money?"

"So I can buy food."

"Why do you want to eat?"

"To live."

"Why do you live?"

With that, the little boy confusedly asked, "Sir, why do I live?"

Sound familiar? This conversation could very well have happened anywhere on the planet, perhaps even in our own hearts. That's because we are all asking the same question, the question of purpose. Rick Warren, for example, obviously hit a nerve when he wrote *The Purpose Driven Life*, an international bestseller. Even many Christians still cannot articulate an answer to the purpose question. And if we can't answer the question for our own lives in our own setting, how could we expect to travel thousands of miles to places like India to answer it for someone else? However, the question of purpose isn't really about figuring out what we're supposed to be *doing*. It's about discovering who we *are*.

Not All Who Believe in God are Worshipers of God

Like me, there are many Christians out there who can identify as a Christian or even a missionary. We often refer to ourselves as *Believers*. Yet what does that mean? James 2:19 says, "Even the demons believe—and shudder." So what separates me from demons if we both believe in the reality of the same God?

Similarly, Romans 1:21 speaks of the lost, "For although they knew God, they did not honor him as God or give thanks to him." That also sounds pretty confusing.

So to be clear, the Bible tells us that there are demons who believe and fear God and that even the lost know God in some way. So what separates the true Believer from these?

Can we say with the priests of old, "You are the Lord, you alone. You have made heaven, the heaven of heavens, with all their host, the earth and all that is on it, the seas and all that is in them; and you preserve all of them; and the host of heaven worships you" (Neh. 9:6)? Can we say with the psalmist, "Oh come, let us worship and bow down; let us kneel before the Lord, our Maker!" (Ps. 95:6)?

Though every knee will eventually bow and every tongue eventually confess Jesus Christ as Lord, it is only those who do their bowing and confessing in this life that will be permitted into God's Kingdom. For those who are in Christ, we are called and compelled toward the one thing that both the demons and the lost cannot even comprehend. As Christians, we are invited to do what we were made to do for Eternity—*worship.*

Now, if you're anything like I was, you're snickering to yourself right now, "Great, we all get to sing four hundred-year-old organ hymns until we're so tired we fall off of our heavenly pews." But that would be the wrong picture of the wrong idea, not to mention the wrong religion. The idea we are going for is intimate relationship, and the picture is somewhere between God's loving embrace and his awesome wonder and majesty. Worship is the expression of a heart of deep, genuine gratitude, not some mundane, mindless mantra.

God has invited us into a relationship in which we know him, love him, and admire him for what he has done for us. God, in his Son Jesus, lived a perfect life and then died on a Cross for you and me and for every sin we've ever committed. Jesus felt the weight of everything foul in this world as he suffered, and that, in fact, *was* his suffering! We couldn't even begin to pay the penalty for one vulgar thought, and yet Jesus paid for all the evils of the world in one cruel moment.

> "For as the earth brings forth its sprouts, and as a garden causes what is sown in it to sprout up, so the Lord God will cause righteousness and praise to sprout up before all the nations" (Isa. 61:11).

This is the work of God, redeeming not just us, but those from every tongue, tribe, and nation to himself (Rev. 14:6). By his grace and through his awesome power, God is rescuing the lost from every corner of the globe and transforming them into true worshipers of himself. The Christian God does not simply impress us with his power like every other world religion; He ransoms us with his blood. Therein lies the paradox of the Christian faith, that God is both humble enough to be reviled and ridiculed on a Roman Cross and yet sovereign enough to command the entire universe.

What's So Great About Heaven?

When we think about God in the context of a loving, redemptive relationship, Heaven seems a lot nearer. Yet there is a veil between this life and the next. 1 Corinthians 13:12 puts it this way, "For now we see in a mirror dimly, but then face to face." And let's keep in mind that looking into a first century mirror was a lot like trying to find your reflection in a soup spoon. So when Paul says "dim," he really means it.

We see so little of God right now in this body of flesh and blood, but it's important to remember that what we do see ought to make us long for him like we long for nothing else. That being said, if God has created a way for us to know him so intimately and so powerfully here on earth, we simply can't even begin to imagine the overwhelming awe and wonder of

God's glory "face to face" in heaven. Thus, heaven is not our goal; Jesus is. Heaven, though no doubt spectacular in itself, is simply the divine meeting place for God and his people.

Why Doesn't Everyone Worship God?

That leaves us with a really important question. "If God is so great and so real, why don't more people worship him?"

This brings us to the heart of Christianity. If we go back to Romans 1, we learn that God reveals Himself in such a way that everyone is seeing at least a part of Him. One well-seasoned missionary, Don Richardson, in his book *Eternity in their Hearts* (a reference to Ecclesiastes 3:11), tells the story of his encounter with various people groups who, unbelieving, were not without many customs, morals, and religious practices that at least somewhat mimicked Christianity. Richardson was able to use these similarities as connecting points in bringing the gospel to previously unreached people groups. No one can deny God in their heart of hearts. Yet not everyone comes to salvation.

That's because salvation is a special work of grace that God does only in those he calls to be his children. Now, the "why some and not others" question is a bit of a mystery as we find out in Romans 9-11. But what we do know is that God is actively drawing people to himself. And though he can and does use many different means to accomplish this, we learn from Scripture (and from experience) that he does have one *primary* vehicle in taking the Good News of salvation to a lost world—us.

Paul puts it this way in Romans 10. "How then will they call on him in whom they have not believed? And how are they to believe in him of whom they have never heard? And how are they to hear without someone preaching? And how are they to preach unless they are sent?" I think you can follow Paul's logic here. Like blind beggars, many are moving through life with deep, pressing questions about the source and meaning of life, yet without the vision to see the answer. Without heavenly intervention, these wanderers might never see the light of day. That is where you and I and countless other brothers and sisters come into play.

The Bible calls us "ambassadors," that is, card-carrying representatives of the Gospel of Jesus to a lost and dying world (2 Cor. 5:20). *We*, therefore, as Christians, are God's chosen means by which the gospel moves forward to the ends of the earth. Paul boasts in Romans 10, "How beautiful are the feet of those who preach the good news!" That's because those beautiful feet are bringing salvation to the lost and, ultimately, leading people into lives (and eternities) of *worship*.

As John Piper so rightly points out, "Missions exist because worship doesn't." Thus, where worship is complete, namely in heaven, there will be no more missions. Yet while we sojourn this earth as sojourners *away* from home, missions will always be a part of God's plan for our lives inasmuch as God desires worship.

But what if we *aren't* preaching the good news? What if, even as Christians, we don't find ourselves truly longing for God and for his Kingdom "on earth as it is in heaven" (Matt. 6:10)?

Worship Misdirected: Idolatry

John Piper goes on to clarify in his book, *Let the Nations Be Glad*, that worship is both the *purpose* and the *fuel* of missions. Consequently, if we have a sharing, or, more broadly, even a sin problem, we ultimately have a *fuel* problem. It's like taking a road trip to the beach. We may know the destination, but if we don't have the fuel to get there, no amount of hoping or wishing or planning is going to move our automobile so much as an inch. Likewise, you won't be getting anywhere filling your tank full of food and water. While that may be fuel for our bodies, our automobiles don't operate that way. We can't use just any fuel; it has to be the *right* fuel.

Our natural tendency is to try to insert physical fuels into a spiritual tank. We gorge ourselves on the latest cultural frills and thrills. Television and video games all too easily replace spiritual disciplines like meditation and solitude. The latest wave of internet chat programs competes with prayer and Bible reading. Then there are the more obvious, devious attractions like pornography, romance novels, drug and alcohol addiction, compulsory lying or theft, and the list goes on. I even read one recent report claiming that pedophilia was just another expression of love and, therefore, perfectly defensible and permissible. Tragically, the world's definition of "life well-lived" continues to shift from what is redemptive and holy to what is perverse and ultimately, destructive.

Romans 1:23 describes such a state of the soul. Rome "... exchanged the glory of the immortal God for images resembling mortal man and birds and animals and creeping things." We could expand that list to include cars, money, entertainment, education, and even things like dreams, goals, family, and religion. Yes, even God's gifts like family and church can be an obstacle if they replace God himself as the center of our affections and our worship.

We were all created with the capacity to worship, and really, we all *do* worship. The difference lies in the *object* of our worship. Even Christians can miss this. For the first part of my Christian life, my object of worship was *service to Christ* and not Christ himself. My loose definition of worship produced in me a Christianity that was lazy, lax, and easy. The world, and the devil, for that matter, had no qualms with me. I was fruitless and barren, a worship center of one that affected no one and nothing. As I mistakenly served Christ for the increased love and acceptance I thought I could earn from him, I was oblivious to God's hunger for my worship and to the guidance of the Holy Spirit.

Instead of being drawn to Christ, I was drawn to the benefits of being a Christian. In a world in which everything from politics to jobs to friendships is largely self-serving, it is easy to project that kind of thinking on Christianity.

Our Highest Pleasure

Too often, we end up settling for the cheap, two-bit imitations of real happiness. The irony is that in a culture so consumed with constantly upping the ante on the highs of temporal pleasures, the highest and most undeniable pleasure of all— Jesus— is a rock of offense (Isa. 8:14; Rom. 9:33; 1 Pet. 2:8). Why?

The world does its best to diminish the difference between true worship and idolatry. Satan would have us believe it is more like splitting hairs, but really, the chasm between these two practices could not be further apart. These are two forks in a road that never converge. One fork is for those stubborn thrill seekers bent on earning and controlling only a perceived happiness, while the other leads to a life of real happiness that is *given*, not acquired. That's because God alone is both our source and our cause for true happiness and contentment.

Our highest calling and our highest pleasure is found in what will always be folly to the world, that is, Jesus himself. Are you lacking in motivation to walk in obedience to Jesus? Are you enticed by the mindless "fun" of a lost world? Is Bible reading a chore instead of a desire? Is it painstaking to get up for church in the morning? Is God just somewhere on the periphery; does he get sidelined all too easily? Has sin taken over in such a way that it seems impossible to get out from under it? Are you driven by a paralyzing hunger for safety and security? Do you constantly feel backed into a corner defending your faith? Do you worry and fret about what tomorrow may bring? Do you question whether you will even see heaven at all?

Is your living characterized by simply trying to keep from dying?

The solution to all these questions is the same—*worship*. But that's easier said than done. Arriving at concepts is much easier than arriving at a real way of life. Thankfully, there are those who have "been there, done that," those who can inspire and encourage with their stories of strength and commitment to God. Yet it may be comforting to know also that these "heroes of the faith" were by no means perfect. Just like us, they were afflicted with faults and failures, with weaknesses and insecurities.

Who are these people, you ask? The full list includes prostitutes, murderers, thieves, drunkards, and persecutors of Christianity. Like us, these were ordinary, if not extraordinarily terrible people. Yet the work of the Holy Spirit is without limits if we put our trust in Jesus. He brings life from death and beauty from ashes. As was the case with the apostle Paul, Christianity's first missionary, a fervent hatred was transformed into an even fiercer love. Even so, the testimonies of those heroes before us are not testimonies of man's resilience, but of the awesome transformational power of God and his Word proclaimed.

DISCUSSION QUESTIONS

- What separates us from demons if we both believe in God?

- If God is really so great, why doesn't everyone worship him?

- What is God's primary vehicle in spreading the Good News?

- What are some of the cultural and personal idols that we worship, and how does this kind of misdirected worship affect our Christian testimony?

MISSIONS AND THE BIBLE

"The Bible is not the basis of missions; missions is the basis of the Bible."
– Ralph Winter

I can remember meeting my first missionary as a young child. He was the guest of honor in my second grade Sunday school class. To be honest, I can't remember a word he said, and I may not have remembered him at all if it weren't for one defining characteristic that both scared me and thrilled me. "Bodie," as he was called, was missing half a finger, and, to top it off, he had lost it in a battle with an Asian snapping turtle. He showed us the photo!

Now, as a young boy, that was enough for me to be "all in." Slaying dragons, karate chopping bad guys, and fighting giant alien turtles were all in a day's work for me. My ten-year-old imagination ran wild with the missionary life, which as far as I could tell, wasn't any different than the life of Tarzan or Huckleberry Finn.

For the next decade, nothing much changed for me. I had traded Huckleberry Finn and Tom Sawyer for a stack of missionary biographies, but unfortunately, I read them much the same—like larger than life adventure stories. With each passing epic saga, I became more and more enchanted—no, in love with the idea of becoming a missionary. Yet my love and enthusiasm for missions sounded all too much like the "noisy gong" or "clanging symbol" Paul describes in 1 Corinthians 13. Paul, in fact, would know just how I felt since his call to missions started very much the same way—with the pursuit of his own agenda and glory. Let me explain.

Saul of Tarsus

The same suffering servant who wrote over half of the books in the New Testament—Paul—was once known as the laudable and legendary, perhaps infamous, I should say, Saul of Tarsus. A true "Hebrew of Hebrews" and Pharisee of Pharisees, as he himself recalled in Philippians, Saul's reputation preceded him. Every man both feared and revered him—the incredibly educated, impeccably obedient, and impressively credentialed—Saul of Tarsus. Yet even with every title and benefit of the age, the great and mighty Saul fell short of the glory of God. In fact, zealous Saul instigated and orchestrated the persecution and even martyrdom of countless new Christians in the first century including the church's first ordained deacon, Stephen.

Yet even Saul, sinner of sinners, was not beyond the reach of God's supernatural and saving grace. In one of the most dramatic conversions of the Bible, Jesus shone down from heaven with a blinding light that changed the course and destination of not only Saul's life but all of Christianity. From that point forward, the mighty Saul would become the humble Paul, Christianity's first and most accomplished missionary. Through harrowing hardships, the Holy Spirit led Paul from one city to the next, joyfully preaching the Word of God at any cost to himself. From jail cells and deep waters, under attack from stones and canes and whips, and sometimes alone and without food or shelter, Paul did not falter in his resolution to see God's Word proclaimed among the nations. Paul put it this way in Acts 20:24, "But I do not account my life of any value nor as precious to myself, if only I may finish my course and the ministry that I received from the Lord Jesus, to testify to the gospel of the grace of God."

Paul's life, even with all the credentials and benefits he had garnered, amounted to nothing, or in Paul's words, something worse than nothing. "But whatever gain I had," Paul says, "I counted as loss for the sake of Christ. Indeed, I count everything as loss because of the surpassing worth of knowing Christ Jesus my Lord. For his sake I have suffered the loss of all things and count them as rubbish, in order that I may gain Christ ..." (Phil. 3:7-8). These are strong words from one of the most privileged men of his time, especially considering Paul wrote the book of Philippians from prison. Far from the jaded, self-pitiable, and depressed character we would expect to find given the circumstances, Paul was a joyful and exuberant encourager to the Philippian church and others.

Yet this transition from Saul to Paul came neither quickly nor easily. For well over a decade after his conversion, Paul disappeared from the scene. Even with Paul's prior Pharisaical knowledge of the Bible, he needed a new and humble beginning which meant sipping on spiritual milk until he was strong enough for meat. Paul was no stranger to the process of sanctification, even as superhuman as he may seem to us now. Putting one foot in front of the other, Paul would have grown slowly and painfully, especially in allowing Christ to cover the weighty burdens of shame and sin. Even with his new heart, Paul struggled to do the things that he ought, and just like you and me, relied daily, even hourly, on the grace of God that empowers and equips for the work of ministry and obedience.

Like myself and others, and like we see in Paul's former life as Saul, the mission of God, as noble as it sounds, can be just another pathway to self-exaltation. For me, missions provided a gateway to adventure in which the stories of epic battles and near-death experiences would be my highest prize. For Paul, a twisted pursuit of perfect lawfulness led him to the life of an assassin in hunting down Christians in the name of Yahweh. Now, in the modern day of technology and accessibility, the temptation is to use especially short-term missions as an all-expenses-paid vacation with all the frills and thrills of international sightseeing. These are but three possibilities in an ocean of deception when it comes to distorting God's mission for personal gain. Whether it is self-glorification (missions as adventure), self-righteousness (missions as earning God's approval), or self-entertainment (missions as hedonism), it is all too easy to contaminate the mission of God with our own fleshly desires. This is why it's important to have a Biblical understanding of missions, because without it, we are prone to endless avenues of self-fulfillment.

Missions in the Old Testament

We often think of missions as being only a New Testament phenomenon, but God's call to missions actually dates all the way back to Abraham in Genesis. The great Abrahamic Covenant was not unlike the New Testament Great Commission. God's promise is coupled with his command to go. "Now the Lord said to Abram, 'Go from your country and your kindred and your father's house to the land that I will show you. And I will make of you a great nation, and I will bless you and make your name great, so that you will be a blessing. I will bless those who bless you, and him who dishonors you I will curse, and in you all the families of the earth shall be blessed.'" With the comfort and assurance of God's promise, Abraham moved forward in faith from his homeland of Haran to the foreign land of Canaan. And as history would have it, God, of course, came through on his promise, to make Abraham the father of the Jewish people and a blessing to all the earth.

From Genesis to Psalms to the writings of the prophets, missions resonate from the pages of the Old Testament. King David's song of praise in 1 Chronicles 16:23-24 is just one example of many. "Sing to the Lord, all the earth! Tell of his salvation from day to day. Declare his glory among the nations, his marvelous works among all the peoples!" God even appointed Jeremiah directly as a "prophet to the nations" (Jer. 1:5).

The message of the New Testament, then, is simply the next chapter in the story. It is not the beginning of a new revelation, but part of the continually unfolding story of God and his mission to expand his Kingdom and glorify his name. We, as his people, are simply invited into that story as chosen ambassadors of his gospel message, and we change the world by his power and not our own.

Whose Story is it Anyway?

Unfortunately, this is a cornerstone truth of Scripture that we often overlook both in theology and practice, that our lives are part of God's story and not the other way around. How many times have we been guilty of trying to incorporate God into the hustle and bustle of our busy lives, as if we are the screenwriters for God's acted script? We demean Almighty God by using him as a sort of benevolent Santa Claus who lavishes good and deserving gifts upon us. Like spoiled little children, we serve the Lord joyfully and dutifully as long as it is on our terms, our time, and costs us little to nothing.

King David's motto, on the contrary, centered on God's worth, not his own. "I will not offer burnt offerings to the Lord my God that cost me nothing" (2 Sam. 24:24). David recognized himself as simply a mere stitch in God's beautiful tapestry. However, in our modern day "me-centered" Christianity, many of us are taught to see ourselves as the entire tapestry. I used to read every "you" in the Bible as "me only." My theology went something like this: Scripture alone, by faith alone, by grace alone, and for me alone. However, in studying the Biblical languages, I came to a profound realization that revolutionized my approach to the Scriptures: the Bible was written to the whole Church ("you" plural), not just to me.

Missions thus became a team activity and not a solo stunt. The fate of the world no longer rested upon my shoulders but on the greatness and sovereignty of God. Acts 17:25 reminded me that God is not "served by human hands, as though he needed anything." Still, God has chosen, by his grace, to commission us, weak and sinful as we may be, to bear his message of grace to the farthest reaches of the globe and to do so with the power and presence of the Holy Spirit working in us, through us, and far beyond us. The only catch is, it's going to cost us.

The Cost of Discipleship

Our culture is obsessed with the easy life. Here in the West, we are born into padded rooms where pain is the most egregious of four-letter words. Disillusioned, we gorge ourselves on the ecstasy of mind-altering substances, entertainment, and self-help therapy as thrill seekers and hedonists, entertaining ourselves at the expense of encountering the fullness of being made in God's image.

For Jesus, God in the flesh, pleasure and pain were by no means mutually exclusive. Nor were they for Peter who encouraged us to "rejoice insofar as you share Christ's suffering" (1 Pet. 4:13). James said, "Count it all joy, my brothers, when you meet trials of various kinds ..." (1:2). Paul also could say, "I rejoice in my sufferings ..." (Col. 1:24). And finally, there was Jesus, our Lord, "... who for the joy that was set before him endured the cross ..." (Heb. 12:2). Let's be clear, though. Suffering is not a possibility; it's a promise.

Paul warned Timothy, "... all who desire to live a godly life in Christ Jesus will be persecuted" (2 Tim. 3:12). And for 176,000 Christians every year, that is a persecution that leads to death. Like Jesus who "... came not to be served but to serve, and to give his life as a ransom for many," there are those who are giving their lives away for the sake of the gospel (Matt. 20:28). And courageously, they stop at nothing and bow to no one in doing it.

As the mountain of Christian persecution around the world continues to grow at record pace, can we say with Paul, "For to me to live is Christ and to die is gain" (Phil. 1:21)? Could we believe Jesus enough that we would lay down our lives in worship—a life that was bought by God at the most precious price imaginable—the blood of His Son? Could our assurance of faith run deep enough to put to death our "confidence in the flesh" in exchange for being "constrained by the Spirit" (Phil. 3:3; Acts 20:22)?

The Great Commission

For those faithful few who are willing to live and die in binding themselves to the promises and commands of the Scriptures, our Savior left us with one final imperative before ascending to the Father—what we know today as *The Great Commission*. "All authority in heaven and on earth has been given to me," Jesus said. "Go therefore and make disciples of all nations, baptizing them in the name of the Father and of the Son and of the Holy Spirit, teaching them to observe all that I have commanded you. And behold, I am with you always, to the end of the age" (Matt. 28:18-20).

Far from separatist holy huddlers or fearful and fleeing deserters, we are "more than conquerors" in Christ Jesus' authority, which he has given us freely and purposefully (Rom. 8:37). We, of all people, ought to march boldly and confidently into the lions' dens of this world to proclaim the good news of Jesus Christ to what may be one of the most self-centered generations to ever walk the planet, 80,000 of whom will die lost today and go to hell forever.

From the perspective of eternity, the difference between life and death is a chasm of more length and depth and width than our human minds could ever fathom, yet daily we bear the fragrance of this weighty truth to lost and found alike (2 Cor. 2:14-17). For many, the intimacy of this weight expresses itself in a deep-rooted compassion for the lost and a fervency to see God's name and attributes proclaimed among neighbors and even nations. For others, a tragic vanity blinds and distracts with the worries and anxieties of a life lived in isolation from the real weight of glory. Neighbors perish and nations pass away without notice as the Word of God stagnates in the hearts of believers who never cultivate a holy passion and urgency for God's Word proclaimed. Fear takes root as love is wasted on the internal trappings of an estranged heart that, at best, might peddle the message of Christ out of guilt or for personal merit.

Such is the state of much of the Western Church. Once a beacon of hope for the nations, the West has crumbled under the weight of secularism and individualism. The Church has splintered under the attack of the bombshells of religious liberalism and materialism. While new converts in China, India, and Africa beg for attention to Great Commission discipleship, our energies are consumed in selling the latest brand of Christianity to a consumer-driven Church that seems to care more for appearance than substance. The global Church today is, in many ways, pressed up against the wall by its own immaturity as the torch of leadership is passed from West to South and East. Even so, the discouragement we are experiencing, especially in the Western Church, is not the ringing of defeat but the growing pangs of a people not yet come to full maturity—and what I believe is a call back to the basic but forgotten discipline of faithful discipleship.

The Great Commission is not merely a call to go but to actively disciple every believer to observe each and every command of God. Yet we are far too contented with Christianity's bare minimums. As C. S. Lewis puts it, "We are half-hearted creatures, fooling about with drink and sex and ambition when infinite joy is offered us, like an ignorant child who wants to go on making mud pies in a slum because he cannot imagine what is meant by the offer of a holiday at the sea. We are far too easily pleased." Yet in being so pleased with so little, as Lewis points out, we miss the unfathomable and indescribable greatness of deeper and deeper revelations of God's love and splendor. And worse still, we are very little compelled to declare the glories of a God whom we scarcely know.

An Invitation

At the 2010 meeting of the Lausanne Movement in Cape Town, one of the commitments made by global church leaders was "the whole church taking the whole gospel to the whole world." The implications of such a statement are voluminous, but one thing is clear: the commitment is total and anything less than that represents an unfinished task. As it stands now, there is a fraction of the church taking a variety of gospels to the easiest and most "reached" parts of the world.

Still, at every stage in church history and even now, there are those precious saints committing themselves to the impossible—going to the hard places with a powerful gospel presentation. And while certainly we owe the spread of the gospel to the mighty work of the Holy Spirit, we also recognize those beautiful feet that the

Spirit has used as vessels to spread God's name and renown.

It is to these missionary greats that we now turn our attention, the ones who carried the mantle of the faith to the farthest reaches of the planet.

DISCUSSION QUESTIONS

- What are three examples of a *poor* motivation to do missions?

- Is missions a part of the Old Testament? How so?

- What is your view of suffering as it relates to the Christian faith?

- Why does the *Great Commission* place such a heavy emphasis on discipleship? Why should we spend time and energy discipling people who are already saved and going to heaven?

MISSIONS AND HISTORY

"The history of missions is the history of answered prayer."
– Samuel Zwemer

The great second-century church father Tertullian is quoted as saying, "The blood of the martyrs is the seed of the Church." That's because Tertullian, like many of the church fathers, was born into an era of persecution, a persecution that the Church endured for its first three hundred years of existence.

Early Church Persecution

The twelve apostles (save Judas, the betrayer) were no exception, though many of their accounts are extra-biblical and not without some suspicion. But as legend, and in some cases, the Bible would have it, Jesus, Andrew, Simon, Bartholomew, Philip, and Peter were all crucified, Peter upside-down. John was boiled and exiled, and his brother, James, was beheaded with a sword as was the apostle Paul. Matthew also was slain with the sword. Thomas was lanced to death and Thaddeus filled with arrows. James, son of Alphaeus, was thrown from the temple and then beaten to death. And the list goes on.

In some cases, newly committed Christians were devoured by animals in Roman gladiator matches, while some, tragically, were burned as human torches. "Others suffered mocking and flogging, and even chains and imprisonment. They were stoned, they were sawn in two, they were killed with the sword. They went about in skins of sheep and goats, destitute, afflicted, mistreated—of whom the world was not worthy—wandering about in deserts and mountains, and in dens and caves of the earth" (Heb. 11:36-38). These early believers courageously bore the gospel message to the borders of the known world, scattering seeds of faith and watering them with their blood into churches that still exist even to this day. Ironically though, it is the Roman army that may have done more for the spread of the gospel than any of the early apostles could have dreamed. What these Roman conquerors meant for evil, God meant for good.

The Fall of Jerusalem

Jesus, as did many of the early apostles, died on a Roman cross, not a Jewish one. That's because although the Jews did have some level of independence, Rome governed much of the known world. But as Roman oppression increased, so did the civil unrest of the Jews until in A.D. 66, Judea was in all out rebellion. Sadly, this small uprising amounted to little more than a splinter in the hand of a great army as Jerusalem fell and the temple with it in A.D. 70.

And while the repercussions of this event were numerous, the most resounding and effectual impact on the world was heard in the diaspora of the first century church. A holy huddle became a church in motion, running for their lives to every corner of the earth and taking with them the Holy Spirit and the message of hope and salvation. The Church began to spread like wildfire along the trade routes and far beyond the reaches of the great Roman Empire, that is, at least until the beginning of the fourth century.

A (Poisoned) Recipe for World Peace

It was in A.D. 313 that Constantine issued the *Edict of Milan*, effectively ending the persecution that Christianity had known for its entire existence. By the end of the fourth century, Christianity would be the official religion of the Byzantine Empire, which encompassed all of the Middle East and much of Asia, Europe, and Africa. Missions would slow and commitment would wane in the coming centuries as Christianity became the status quo. In this new world, with all of the benefits and none of the costs associated with Christianity's first three centuries, the Christian faith was all of a sudden appealing, even advantageous. In a word, Christianity, for the first time, was in danger of becoming *nominal*. Still, this nominalism was only a symptom of a much wider epidemic, that is, Constantine's prescription for peace: the union of church and state.

This opened the door to all kinds of corruption of the religious authority as churchmen began climbing the corporate ladder, so to speak. Popes would eventually crown kings as pious power seekers slowly displaced government officials as heads or at least joint-heads of state. The church would also eventually become the greatest land owner in Europe. This "success," however, if it can be called that, was not immediate as a great nemesis would first encroach on the Christian heartland.

The Birth of Islam

What first began as Christian heresy would quickly explode into a full scale religion encompassing the whole of the Christian world. Well before the end of the Middle Ages in the fifteenth century, Christianity would become the world's only displaced major religion. As violence, prejudice, and government sanctions against Christians spread across the historic lands of Christianity and Judaism, Christians were forced to retreat northward and westward into Europe while a crescent moon rose over the freshly conquered Middle East where it has remained even to today. Though somehow, Islam's reputation would not be marred by its bloody conquest of Christian lands, the world would forever remember one of Christianity's darkest hours in mission gone wrong—the Crusades.

The Crusades: Mission Gone Wrong

In an effort to retake the newly conquered birthplace of Christianity, the church, infused with the power and wealth of the Byzantine Empire, raised its own standing army. Under the banner of the cross and all kinds of counterfeit promises of forgiveness and heavenly merit, the church's mercenary army marched southward in pursuit of Jerusalem and the Muslim armies who defended it. The two hundred- year series of battles that ensued from the eleventh through the thirteenth centuries proved to be as fruitless as they were ill-conceived. The Crusaders came home shamed and defeated, leaving Christianity's hotly contested Holy Land to the jihadists who had long since decided and declared that there would be no room for Christianity on their freshly conquered blood-stained soil. The Crusades would be a hard lesson for a corrupted church in trading a noble *Great Commission* for the vile pursuit of vengeance, land, and riches.

After the Crusades, the church would continue to slay its orthodox theology for the rewards of greater power and influence. The chasm between priest and laity now seemed wider than ever as the church's abuses of authority were directed toward its own naïve constituents. Tragically, the church's great architectural masterpieces of the late Middle Ages were built on the backs of those poor, naïve souls who, under the leadership of the church, quite literally bought into the church's grotesque practice of selling heavenly merit. A return to orthodoxy was clearly in order, and it would come in the form of a fiery monk named Martin Luther.

The Protestant Reformation

It wasn't until the early sixteenth century that the highly spirited Protestant Reformation would emerge as the great return to Biblical purity in both theology and practice. Martin Luther would assume the helm when he posted his *Ninety-five Theses* on the door of the church at Wittenberg in 1517. Ulrich Zwingli, and later John Calvin and others would also carry the torch in both returning to a Christianity that is accessible for the everyday believer and combatting the exploitations and manipulations of the institutionalized Roman Church. The Bible was translated into the vernacular, an orthodox theology of justification was reaffirmed, and the Protestant Church was born, among other things.

However, this miraculous and long overdue turning point in the history of Christianity would bear little fruit in the realm of missions for quite some time. Ironically, it was the Catholic Church, from which the Protestant Church broke away, that would lead the charge in every direction, though mostly on the shoulders of colonialism and oftentimes for the purpose of hindering a rapidly expanding Protestantism.

The Catholic Monastics

Catholic monastics were at the forefront of this charge, most notably the Jesuits under the leadership of founder Ignatius Loyola and comrade Francis Xavier. Cast in droves to the Americas and the Far East, these monastics left no stone unturned in dispersing across lands and nations that were largely unknown to Western Europe. The multi-functioning mission station became the norm as a system of commerce to operate monasteries, schools, hospitals, and business incubators in one central location. Many of these communities thrived, but the threat of tyranny was also close at hand with newly-established colonial governments who were more eager to exploit than to proselytize.

The Protestant Missionary Movement

Eventually, the Protestant missions movement would also find some traction. The French Huguenots and the Moravians were marvelous forerunners of this movement, the latter generally being the more highly regarded of the two. The Moravians especially were one of the most zealous bands of missionaries that Christianity has ever seen. They began a twenty-four hour prayer chain in 1727 that lasted for over one hundred years. The Moravians were also bold enough to pack their earthly goods into coffins in venturing out on their missionary journeys, never expecting to return home. And while the Moravians and their leader, Count Zinzendorf, were unparalleled missions movers and thinkers in their time, it is William Carey who has been esteemed the title "Father of Modern (Protestant) Missions."

A gifted Englishman who aptly and skillfully served the Indian nation as doctor, scientist, shoemaker, business entrepreneur, and diplomat, William Carey was most notably a linguist. During his tenure in India, Carey oversaw the translation of forty-four languages and dialects, effectively opening the gospel to millions upon millions. Like the Moravians before him, the success of Carey's mission lay in his total, and in his case, life-long commitment to it. Carey would bury two wives and three children in India, and while far from unaffected, Carey refused to allow the tragedies of life in a fallen world to deter him from his heavenly callings and purposes.

With the notoriety and success of Carey and others, the Protestant missionary movement in Europe would quickly spread across the Atlantic to North America. Adoniram Judson would be the first from the United States but others would soon follow.

Modern Day Missions

The nineteenth and early twentieth centuries would be marked by the emergence of whole missionary movements including all kinds of mission societies, organizations, and denominational mission boards, one of the most notable being the *Student Volunteer Movement* in the United States which was founded in 1886. This was, not coincidentally, just two years after the *Cambridge Seven* including pioneer missionary C. T. Studd had organized their mission from England to China. Young people across America, inspired by those before them and by their counterparts in Western Europe, united together to spur one another on toward the completion of the *Great Commission*. With little, if any, formal training in Bible, missions, linguistics, or anthropology, students traded the comfort and familiarity of home for the challenges and hardships of romance turned reality in often hostile and primitive lands. Scores of these missionaries died within their first year on the mission field or even en route. The unbridled passion of these masses of young people would need the halter of wisdom and knowledge, but that would come only with experience.

As missions progressed over the course of the twentieth century, the same mission organizations that had earlier sprung up with zeal and enthusiasm alongside the *Student Volunteer Movement* also became the think tanks and training grounds of modern missions. Strategies developed as those pioneer missionaries who had survived and endured now decades of missionary service began to return home with the wealth of wisdom that can only come with age and experience. Books and pamphlets were written; seminars were planned as both Biblical and practical training became an increasingly integral part of missionary preparation.

Global Christians

Eventually, the entire world would come together on this important issue of missions, most notably in recent years through the *Lausanne Movement* which began with American evangelist Billy Graham's call to global leaders to evangelize. A group of 2700 delegates from over 150 nations met in 1974 at the first assembly in Lausanne, Switzerland, and the movement has only gained momentum from there. At the 2010 gathering in Cape Town, South Africa, there were over 4000 delegates from 198 nations, this time with a much larger proportion from the developing world.

Also at the cutting edge of this new movement has been the *US Center for World Mission* founded by the late Ralph Winter. In large part to the efforts of Dr. Winter and his comrades, the church has begun to be populated with what we would call "Global Christians," that is, those who possess the passion, vision, and knowledge to make them strategic and effective disciples of Christ in a diverse world of ever-changing cultural landscapes. Through training programs like *Perspectives on the World*

Christian Movement and research projects such as the *Joshua Project*, the *US Center for World Mission* is both anthropologically articulating the degree of Christian presence in every people group on the planet and mobilizing and training a generation to be effective cross-cultural witnesses. The resources they have been able to provide and the unified front they have been able to organize are providing a rich and extensive framework for moving forward in mission into the twenty-first century.

I had the privilege of meeting with Dr. Winter just months before he died in 2009 when our paths crossed in the small port city of Pohang, South Korea, of all places. Though I gladly would have spent the next week or more with Dr. Winter to glean the riches of wisdom from this seasoned sage of the faith, I was allotted only a taxi ride and dinner. I surprised myself with how carefully I scrutinized this man whom I had come to respect as an almost demi-god with all he had accomplished in the realm of mission. My scrutiny, however, did nothing but bring me back to planet earth as I beheld the plainness of speech, dress, and even personality of this great man of faith. His simple and humble demeanor was a testimony not to himself but to the greatness of God to use whomever he chooses to accomplish the great tasks of this world. While I did have some specific questions for Dr. Winter, which he graciously and enthusiastically answered, I realized that, above all, Dr. Winter was an empowerer whose interest was not in offering me clever stories and anecdotes as a sort of Christian roadside assistance, but in boldly and straightforwardly catapulting me forward to live fervently the life God intended for me. I entered my meeting thinking what the world needs is more Dr. Winters but left with a strong sense that the power of the Holy Spirit is available to transform any one of us including myself into God's agents of radical transformation.

This is the great lesson we learn from Christian history, that God chose to use ordinary men and women in extraordinary ways and that both the ends and the means are for God's glory and his glory alone. Therein also lies our challenge, that in reaching for the stars, we don't strive for our own profit "but for him who for [our] sake died and was raised" (2 Cor. 5:15).

DISCUSSION QUESTIONS

- How is it that, as Tertullian said, "The blood of the martyrs is the seed of the church?" Why would church growth accelerate in seasons of persecution and slow in seasons of prosperity?

- How was the fall of Jerusalem in A.D. 70 instrumental in expanding the church?

- Discuss the pros and cons of the separation of church and state, especially as it relates to the age from Constantine until the Protestant Reformation?

- What is a *Global Christian*?

- Why is Christian history relevant for us today?

GLOBAL CHRISTIANITY

"In the vast plain to the north I have sometimes seen, in the morning sun, the smoke of a thousand villages where no missionary has ever been."
– Robert Moffat

I can remember some time ago visiting one of the great megachurches of the southern United States in Birmingham, Alabama. There in the buckle of the "Bible Belt," as it's called, church spires outnumber people, or so it seemed. With congregations meeting on literally every street corner, I have heard that Birmingham has the greatest density of churches of any city in the world. That is why I was particularly surprised the Sunday I paid a visit to this local epicenter church.

Arriving alone after an exceptionally tiring weekend of meetings and socials, I strategically chose an unsuspecting seat in the middle of the elaborate football stadium—I mean—sanctuary (though in a room full of 5,000 people, every seat is amply unsuspecting). Though I appreciate the church as a wonderful source of relationships, I have to admit that this particular Sunday, especially as a socially exhausted out-of-town visitor, I was not exactly the epitome of friendliness. I spread my arms around the chairs to my side to reinforce what I had come to understand as the unofficial "one chair in between us" rule, just to make sure. As the service began, I assumed the "I'm praying, don't talk to me" position, clasping both hands under my bowed head, but in the process, I thoughtlessly left my flanks unguarded. As I lifted my head to resume the "one chair inbetween us" position, I realized I was too late. There he sat, grinning from cheek to cheek and eager for my time and attention. To make matters worse, halfway through the service, he started to cry. I sensed a sermon illustration coming on.

The mysterious intruder turned out to be a missionary, though by the looks and sounds of him, he was most definitely *not* from Alabama. But as I listened to my newfound friend speak, my dry bones began to rattle.

Akiki (meaning "friend"), let's call him, was from Uganda, where over one third of the population is living on less than $1.25 per day. His family and his church were not of means, to be sure, but when they committed themselves to sending their first missionary, what they lacked in finances they more than made up for in their overwhelming resolve. Akiki began to relay his story.

As Akiki's home church was commissioning him for the mission field, his pastor asked for an offering with which to send him. The congregation emptied their pockets of whatever they had, but when it arrived on the altar, it was not enough. Each member then went home to pack extra clothes and possessions and laid those on the altar as well, but still, it was not enough. Finally, the congregation went home and brought back with them their animals and livestock, sacrificing, in faith, their daily bread in exchange for the hope of salvation for lost souls. With the knowledge that his brothers and sisters in Christ would lay down their very lives to support him, Akiki left for the mission field of the United States of America, the largest mission sending country on the planet.

Akiki's story left me speechless, guilt-stricken, bewildered, amazed—altogether wrestling with a bizarre mix of emotions. First of all, I simply couldn't wrap my arms around that kind of sacrifice and commitment, no matter how hard I tried; I was in awe.

Secondly, why would Akiki come here? Don't we send plenty of missionaries to Africa without them coming here to the US? I thought missions was from "the West to the rest," as it has been said.

From Everywhere to Everywhere

There is a new paradigm for missions on the horizon, and it goes something like this: *missions from everywhere to everywhere.* Missions is no longer just a Western responsibility; it's a global partnership. The United States, for example, the largest missions-sending country in the world, is now also the largest receiving country for missionaries. Like Akiki, men and women from around the globe are sacrificially and steadfastly committing themselves to what many hope will be a reformation of one of the straying epicenters of modern day Christianity.

But rather than mourn the decline of Christianity in Europe and North America, like many are prone to do, we must recognize that God has a sovereign plan to bring the gospel to every people group in the world. Epicenters may shift from one place to another, but that's nothing new. Christianity has always been a religion on the move, and it continues to expand, now more than ever.

Christianity's Shifting Epicenter

We have to remember that Christianity began as a Middle Eastern religion with a limited global reach. Expelled first by Rome and then by Islam, Christianity then moved north and west to Europe during the Middle Ages, but it was humanism and secularism that caught up with it there. In time, Christianity would retreat still further west to the populace of North America, but unfortunately, it brought its parasites with it. Both humanism, secularism, and add to that materialism, continue to take their toll on the church of North America today.

Now the shift is to the Global South and East. The churches of Africa, Latin America, and Asia are exploding. Some estimate, for example, that in China up to 30,000 people are becoming Christians every day, and not coincidentally, as we have learned, this is also one of the most persecuted Christian populations on earth. Many churches continue to meet underground for fear of imprisonment, torture, or even death. Still, there are almost as many evangelicals in China as there are in the United States.

In India also, tens of thousands are coming to Christ every day, many of whom are initially drawn through dreams, signs, and wonders. In a land where spiritualism is very much part of the cultural and religious DNA, God is doing great miracles of faith through bold witnesses proclaiming the Word of God. The religious extremism of Hindus and Muslims, though very much a threat, has not deterred believers in India from making a great impact on their nation.

Africa, like India, is also a land alive with animism and spiritualism where miracles are woven into the fabric of the Christian faith. Just the sheer numbers of Christians there alone is a miracle in itself. In fact, it won't be long until Africa is home to more Christians than any other continent on the planet. And ironically, Africa's theology tends to be much more conservative and orthodox than that of Europe or North America, hence the large number of African "reformers" leaving as missionaries to the Western world.

Even in predominantly Muslim lands where believers are still intensely persecuted, Christianity is surging. Behind closed doors, an underground church thrives. In Indonesia, for example, the most populous Muslim country on earth, two million people convert from Islam to Christianity every year. The Christian population in the Arab Middle East is also, perhaps surprisingly, on the rise, though not without immense sacrifice on behalf of our brothers and sisters there.

Thus, while the churches in Europe and North America continue to decline, most of the world is experiencing exponential growth. But let's not write off the role of the West just yet, not by any means. New movements and new paradigms both for church and missions are springing up in Western nations as the Church, very much still alive, especially in the United States, continues to use its historic gifts of creativity, entrepreneurialism, and invention to further expand the Kingdom of God.

The Church in the West

Right now, 127,000 of the world's approximately 400,000 long-term missionaries are sent from the United States, making the US the largest mission sending country in the world. This doesn't include the one to four million Americans going on *short-term* mission trips every year. Also, the vast majority of the world's major missions organizations have home bases in Western nations that provide the backbone of wisdom, experience, financing, and manpower for global missions.

Furthermore, almost half of the world's Christian wealth is still in the hands of Americans and a significant portion of the second half in the hands of Western

Europeans. The wealth of Western nations remains unprecedented. But this wealth has also been a curse that has stricken us with the increasingly serious pandemic of material idolatry. We have to admit that with all the manpower and resources we have, if our churches here in the West were as sacrificial as Akiki's little congregation in Uganda, the Great Commission would have been fulfilled decades if not centuries ago.

The Great Western "Piggy Bank"

Let's not reduce the West either to a mere missions "piggy bank" of sorts, as some have been wont to do. Unfortunately, there is a growing movement to demean and demote Western Christians to mere financiers in funding the developing world's "real" work of ministry on the front lines. And while it's true that local or native missionaries (who know the indigenous language and culture) are more naturally equipped to minister to their own people than any Western foreigner, there are still over three thousand unreached, unengaged people groups. This means that there is not a single local witness or foreign missionary present among those peoples. Thus, the era of missions is not over, not for anyone, and especially not for Western nations either as senders or goers.

God's Ultimate Plan for the Nations

God's sovereign plan for the nations is being unfolded in his time, and he has promised us that representatives from every nation, tribe, people, and language will be gathered around the throne of Heaven. We can, therefore, rest on God's promises, praying in faith for the day when his promises should be fulfilled.

In the meantime, it is our duty, our pleasure, and our holy command to participate in God's Great Commission, engaging the lost on a global scale, each in our own role as God has called and equipped us.

DISCUSSION QUESTIONS

- How has the epicenter of Christianity changed over the last two thousand years? Where is it shifting now?

- What do you think is causing Christianity's center to shift?

- Though we didn't articulate it in this chapter, what do you think are some of the factors that have contributed to the decline of Christianity in Western nations?

- Does the Western Church still have a role in missions? What is it?

- What are some ways you can be involved in global missions?

PART 2:
ON THE MISSION

BEING THE GOSPEL

"The spirit of Christ is the spirit of missions. The nearer we get to Him, the more intensely missionary we become."
– Henry Martyn

Those outside of Christ will inevitably possess a spirit that shakes with at least some degree of uncertainty in their heart of hearts. The challenge for the believer is to allow that spiritual unrest to be the wedge that splits those calloused hearts and not the wedge that compromises the gospel's proclamation.

The Way of the World

Modernism tells us that there is an explanation to everything, that science may be the god we are looking for in explaining to us, in full, all we could possibly hope to know. From it, we are offered Sir Isaac Newton's third law of motion which states decidedly that "to every action, there is an equal and opposite reaction."

In similar fashion, the concept of "karma," at least in principle, is a cornerstone to every major world religion—Buddhism, Hinduism, Islam, and others. In this system of rewards and retributions, for every cause, there is an equal effect, and to an equal degree of either good or evil. Each one is the master of his own destiny in trying to manipulate the gods for personal benefit.

Such is the dark reality for the unchristian world.

But what if that world were turned over on its head? What if we, like Paul, rallied against our Lord only to find ourselves embraced by that which we sought to condemn? What if our cruelty was rewarded with favor and our oppression with kindness? What if our bitterness was met with patience and our hatred with steadfast love? What if, independent of our fruitless strivings, there was a path to perfect righteousness?

Such is the hope for untold billions—if they only knew.

The Gospel

There was once, and just once, one who sought only our goodness. Born in a farm stall, he made his first bed in a feeding trough—a man of humble beginnings and even humbler endings. Though a carpenter by trade, what he built with his hands was of no consequence compared to what he accomplished through his broken body and his blood poured out. Born to die and dying to be made alive again, his mission was of monumental significance, and yet he was a man of no reputation. He spent himself teaching peace, forgiveness, and compassion, healing the sick and lame, visiting orphans and widows, entertaining children, dining with prostitutes—loving the unlovable and forgiving the unforgivable—bringing hope to the hopeless and good gifts to those who hardly deserved them.

Nevertheless, even with nobility of mission and character, there were those who hated him. How many times would he have looked into the eyes of those who reviled him, and how grieved would he have been at their mistrust—their unbelief? Yet how fervently did he pray for their forgiveness, even in his final and most scathing moments. With imminent death creeping forward ever so fiercely and life ebbing away into history, his last words, mustered through the most holistic suffering imaginable, were those of forgiveness.

And while the Jewish religious leaders rallied in pride at the sight of his motionless body strung high upon a cross, Heaven began to chime the wedding bells in those final moments before the groom would bring home his bride. The most catastrophic moment in history was only the beginning of what would prove to be the most earth shattering victory for those who *did* believe in the man who could not be defeated, not even by death.

And though his bride would not receive him, he ransomed her with his life, and for all eternity. Her stubbornness and her refusal were of no consequence to the one who loved her, because his love was not contingent upon her—it couldn't be. She was nothing to behold, unsightly in all her ways, in fact nothing more than a corpse, and yet she was more loved than she would ever be able to fathom. She would enjoy the love and forgiveness that knows no bounds—through the only one who offers it—Jesus.

False "Gospels"

Yet not every "gospel" sounds quite like this one. There are countless varieties. But let's be clear: any deviation from the biblical gospel account is not merely an alternative route or a subtle detour—it is simply not the gospel at all.

Sadly, we as believers can be our own worst enemies. The compromised testimonies of those unchecked, unguarded, and oftentimes undiscipled believers can be the greatest deterrent of all. These minimalist Christians bear little resemblance to Jesus, especially in the fruit they yield, and they are polluting the way others are retelling the gospel story. In the end, the gospel can be so belligerently undefined in its proclamation that it is reduced to little more than just another ineffectual fairy tale. Tragically, the poor hearers of such "gospels" may live and die never knowing more than a fantastical tale that some sloppy sheep conveniently invented and called "gospel."

Even worse, there are entire churches and even denominations propagating such "gospels." Instead of being a launching pad for the mission of God, these liberal religious perversions of the gospel simply inflate our egos until we forget our embarrassing record of weakness and defeat. This is "the temptation of this age," as Brennan Manning said, "to look good without being good."

Sacrificing gospel living on the altar of reputation and "success," these countless masses of churchgoers are cowering and retreating to what they feel is a safe middle ground between Jesus and the world. Their lives are wasted on the frivolity of comfort, ease, and entertainment. The average American, for example, now spends over ten years in an average lifespan watching television, and ironically, while the church hardly seems to notice. The degree to which we live our lives vicariously through staged adventures of mindless comedy, sport, and reality television is one of the most embarrassing and yet somehow acceptable travesties of our time, not to mention a devastating Christian testimony to the watching world.

The unfortunate reality is that there is no middle ground between heaven and earth, and those who think they've found it are actually right in the heart of Enemy territory. Like the Church at Laodicea in Revelation 3, especially in prosperous times, the temptation is toward a lukewarm Christianity that is comfortable, easy, and safe. But inasmuch as Jesus threatened to vomit the Church at Laodicea out of His mouth, it seems that Laodicean Christianity is really no Christianity at all.

Gospel Heroes

On the contrary, Christianity is painful, costly, and dangerous, and no one knows that better than Jesus himself, the only one who endured temptation, suffering, and loss to its fullest and most holistic extent. Jesus never traded obedience to his Father for an easier life.

And let's also remember that there are those saints in this world who sing hymns from jail cells and hold prayer vigils from dark underground caves and secret cellars. Many of them will be dead by day's end, almost five hundred to be exact. Yet, like Paul, the sufferings of their "...present time are not worth comparing with the glory that is to be revealed..." (Rom. 8:18). In both life and death, these bright stars reside in the presence of their beloved Savior, who is both their battle cry on earth and their eternal reward in heaven.

The Way of the Gospel

I picture the trench warfare of World War I. The battle lines might not change for months, though the fighting ensued. In one particular series of battles, the battles for Ypres in Belgium, the trench warfare lasted for the better part of three years with little movement by either army. Particularly in the wet marshland of Ypres, men would hunker down in swampy muck pits for months at a time, trying desperately to stay awake and alive in holding their ground against the constant enemy barrage.

It has wisely been said that such times do not make or break a man—they reveal him. How many men would be tempted to abandon their positions for a warm meal and a dry bed? Yet how resentfully might they be remembered, especially when their revealed cowardice would have compromised the success and even the very lives of fellow countrymen still steadfastly fighting on the line? And, conversely, what of those epic warriors, who, though not unscathed by the battle, rally for all they're worth in staying the course? These are revealed for the lion-hearts that they are.

And what of us? How might we be revealed? How *are* we being revealed? Are we sturdy bulwark oaks, steady in the winds of hardship and suffering, or are we seedlings in a shallow soil, uprooted by the gentlest of breezes.

The Gospel Challenge

This leads us to what may be the single biggest challenge in the Western Church today: we want all of the benefits of Christianity without any of the costs, at least not to us. As Jesus' "fair weather friends," we are reminiscent of the early disciples, ready to be Kingdom lords but not Kingdom slaves. Like Peter, we are quick to boast, "Even though they all fall away, I will not ... If I must die with you, I will not deny you" (Mark 14:29, 31). Then, much as those self-proclaimed stalwarts in the Garden of Gethsemane, we can be guilty of sleeping on the job and abandoning our post at the first sight of danger.

Yet, let's also keep in mind that these same cowardly disciples were extraordinarily transformed. They would eventually become the church's first martyrs, proclaiming the gospel at all cost.

The truth is, we only proclaim what we value. So the more we value Jesus, the more we value his mission. The more we value his mission, the more zeal we will have in completing it (and the less excuses in avoiding it). To be clear, we cannot value Jesus and not his mission.

Heart *and* Hands

We are beneficiaries of God's promises, to be sure, but we are also ambassadors of His love. To be *in* Christ is always to be *for* Christ. In fact, the apostle Paul tells us that being *for* Christ was built into the very fabric of our salvation. "...[Christ] died for all, that those who live might no longer live for themselves but for him who for their sake died and was raised" (2 Cor. 5:15). Thus, to reap the benefits of Christ without taking part in Christ's mission is not only paradoxical, it's impossible.

A heart without hands is what the apostle James called *dead* and *useless* (2:20, 26). And while those are pretty strong words, Jesus actually made the dividing line even clearer. "Whoever is not with me," he said, "is against me, and whoever does not gather with me scatters" (Luke 11:23). In other words, standing around on the sidelines is simply not an option. In fact, we are already on the playing field whether we like it or not. As Henri Amiel said, "Every life is a profession of faith, and exercises an inevitable and silent influence." The question is not whether or not we will choose to represent Jesus to the world; it is what that testimony will be.

Gospel Encouragement

Why not let the world see that, despite the potential for pain, we would freely share our love with a lost and lonely world, meeting people in the hard places and rescuing them from their misplaced strivings and misguided affections?

And what if, in reaching out, we were despised, rejected, and reviled? What if, for all our strivings in love, we were cast out in hate? Then our testimony would be no different from our Lord's, who warned us, "If the world hates you, know that it has hated me before it hated you ... If they persecuted me, they will also persecute you" (John 15:18, 20). But what is that compared to eternity with Jesus?

DISCUSSION QUESTIONS

- What is the gospel?

- What are some fears and distractions in sharing the gospel? How might these affect the way you share the gospel?

- How is your everyday behavior a testimony to the gospel? What can you do to increase the effectiveness of your testimony?

- Can we love Jesus without being a part of his mission? Why? How is our engagement of this mission revelatory of our hearts?

SENDER OR GOER

*"You can go, you can send,
or you can disobey."
– John Piper*

We cannot help but be awed and inspired by the iconic heroes of Hollywood, history, and folklore—King Arthur, William Wallace, Robin Hood—just to name a few. The Old Testament greats— Joshua, Samson, Gideon, and King David would also top the list. That's because God created us for dominion over the earth and with the instinct to protect and defend what we hold most dear both in person and principle.

Yet, where would King Arthur be without his knights? And where would William Wallace be without the Scottish army? For every epic champion, there is a trail of sacrificial lambs that helped create the lion and lead him to victory. In modern warfare, for example, for every one man engaged in battle, there are nine supporting. On top of that, there are countless contractors growing food, manufacturing weapons, shipping supplies, providing intelligence, and the list could go on.

The point is that not everyone is a guts and glory front-line warrior. The greatness of an army is measured by the sum of its parts, not simply by the courage of its champion few.

Where do *I* fit in?

Likewise, we as believers are part of a whole—the Church. Each has been endowed with various gifts, abilities, and desires. It can be a mystery how all these elements fit together into some kind of calling or vocation, but the important thing is that they do. Still, it can take time, energy, prayer, self-examination, and some help from the outside to discern exactly what our role is meant to be.

It's true that any one of us could do a great number of things to improve the world, and with all the needs out there, the thought of choosing something specific can be overwhelming. It's easy to simply jump headlong into the first opportunity that comes our way. After all, we're filling a need, aren't we?

However, many of us know the agony of striving outside of what we were really meant to be and do, fretting over what was never our work to begin with. Maybe we were guilted into filling a need, or perhaps we followed a person or a paycheck into a job or ministry opportunity that was never meant to be.

In the end, the vice of compromise is always a life-stealer, often leaving our fiery vigor little more than a match flame. But perhaps we may be asking the wrong question.

The great civil rights leader and theologian Howard Thurman put it this way, "Don't ask yourself what the world needs. Ask yourself what makes you come alive and go do it. Because what the world needs is people who have come alive." In other words, God gave us passions for a reason. As we pursue him and fulfill our God-given passions, we can trust God for how that fits into his sovereign plan for not just us, but for the Church as a whole.

The Bible describes this process in 1 Corinthians 12:4-7. "Now there are varieties of gifts, but the same Spirit; and there are varieties of service, but the same Lord; and there are varieties of activities, but it is the same God who empowers them all in everyone. To each is given the manifestation of the Spirit for the common good."

Is Everyone a Missionary?

When we apply this passage to missions, we understand that God has required and gifted all believers everywhere to be *involved* in missions, but he has not required that each fulfill the role of a missionary.

Let's think back to Jesus' last words on earth, what we have come to call the *Great Commission* (Matt. 28:18-20). Jesus commanded us, "Go ... and make disciples of all nations." Similarly, in Acts 1:8, Jesus also charged us to be his "witnesses ... to the end of the earth." The universality of these commands is total. Our role in fulfilling them, however, is another story. Not everyone's role will be the same just as not everyone's gifts are the same—and that's okay. In fact, that's by sovereign design.

Yet, let's be clear also that there are a variety of gifts and roles within missions itself. But generally speaking, God has established one primary identifying gift for missionaries, especially missionary leaders.

The Gift of Apostleship

The gift of apostleship is the supernatural ability to cross cultures and other barriers as in pioneering the gospel into new places, new situations, and among new peoples. Entrepreneurial, driven, and visionary, these people often find themselves in leadership roles as church planters, movement frontrunners, and event organizers. They are the energetic movers and shakers that may think and act independently but also delight in unifying a team for a common purpose.

This gift is not to be confused with the *office* of Apostle which God appointed to those who were eyewitnesses of Jesus and who were also the authoritative, inspired authors of the New Testament gospel message. This office is not available for us today. Paul and Peter, however, were both appointed to the office of Apostle and endowed with the gift of apostleship. They serve as examples to us today in the use of this gift.

Yet, even given this primary missionary gift, we must also recognize that God is using people with a diversity of gifts and backgrounds on the mission field. Tradesmen, teachers, counselors, medical personnel and virtually any other profession can be found on the mission field—all in different but important capacities. Missionaries are often multi-talented as many missionary posts necessitate it, especially those in the developing world where there are limited resources and personnel.

Still, even though giftedness is a valid and important concern in considering the missionary life, the more essential factor is the missionary *call*.

Missionary Calling

I heard a pastor once say that nine out of ten Christians who claim to have a calling to missions never actually make it to the field long-term. Now even if that's only half true, that's quite troubling. Furthermore, of those who have the courage to attempt a long-term stay, few have the endurance to make it full-term. Many who commit to years leave after only months.

Now there could be any number of reasons for this, but the vast majority of these mission failures can be grouped into three potentially overlapping categories.

The Not-So Called

First, there are those who were never called in the first place. Discernment does not always come quickly or easily. Discerning a call to missions requires: time in prayer and sensitivity to the Spirit of God, the identification and cultivation of gifts and passions attributed to missions, a keen awareness of God's Word concerning missions, an identification with modern day missionaries as well as with the historic and biblical missionary accounts, and the exhortation of fellow believers, especially those charged with our leadership and oversight such as small group leaders and pastors. If few to none of these factors were present, I would seriously question a missionary call.

Many Christians who have no regard for missions or evangelism travel to foreign lands under the auspices that simply being present on the mission field will melt their hearts and transform their gifts and spirits. And while the sights and smells of a new land may be exhilarating and impactful at some level, the mission field itself doesn't actually make missionaries. God makes missionaries. Unfortunately, more often than not, these self-appointed, often short-term "missionaries" do more harm than good and can also be a nuisance to local long-term missionary staff.

The Not-So Committed

The second reason for a failed mission attempt is lack of commitment. For many, the initial thrill and intrigue of international travel and every new and exciting feature that comes with it, is enough to get them to the field and even sustain them for a few months. The novelty of missions, the heroism, the adventure—all of these can be appealing and even sustaining temporarily, but all of these collapse with time. In the end, the commitment is not to a people, a place, an idea, or a task. The commitment is to God, and he is the only one who can sustain. All other commitments will fail save that one.

We can think of our commitment to missions like marriage. Marriage is, above all, a covenant. If we base our marriage on anything else—emotions, passions, lust, goodness—even love—marriage will inevitably fail. It can only be based on a supernatural covenant with God and with each other.

I can remember barely lasting a week in Asia before my first breakdown as I buckled under the weight of even the *thought* of my commitment there. Then, at three to four months, a holy terror set in as I realized that eastern Asia was now home. The food wasn't tasting quite as delicious as I remembered, and the people were growing more irritable. Tasks became more strenuous, and problems became exaggerated.

In reality, nothing outside me had changed; everything was still the same. It was me that had changed. One would expect that a missionary would simply get more and more used to a new life and culture, but it doesn't quite work that way. The rose-colored glasses have to come off before any real cultural understanding can begin. I had to let go of a lifetime of ideals—myself, my culture, my definition of work and missions—all kinds of ideals that I never knew I had. Like sanctification, it is a process that's never complete, but there is always a definitive breaking point in every missionary's journey in which they have to psychologically cross the border that they physically crossed already. But make it over this hump, which is usually a matter of months into an assignment, and there is great hope for staying the full course.

The Not-So Nice

Though really just one obstacle among many in commitment to the mission field, I include this third failure—team conflict—because it is the most highly cited reason for missionaries leaving the field.

Especially in this day and age in which mission teams are increasingly multicultural, we have to keep a keen ear to the ground to really wrap our arms around every dynamic of team function. The way we address each other, how we think and articulate points of tension, our style of management and leadership, and our submission to authority can all be potential pitfalls. Even among Christians (just read the book of Acts), togetherness can create tension.

That's why it's important to, as the book of James warns us, "... be quick to hear, slow to speak, slow to anger" (1:19).

Communication is key and, furthermore, in a way that is culturally appropriate. One must listen for understanding and not for ammunition.

Practicing team building exercises, meeting for regular worship and fellowship, eating meals together, and also protecting each other's rest are all great ways to promote team unity. But at the end of the day, a little humility will go a long way.

The Missions Sender

If, after all things considered, crossing cultural boundaries is simply not your cup of tea, then you, by default, are what we call a missions *sender.* Equally as worthy and essential to God's plan of redemption is supporting those whom God has called to go.

Paul asks in Romans 10:15, "And how are they to preach unless they are sent?" We know from the Scriptures that the early Apostles and even Jesus were all supported by the wealth, prayers, encouragement, and fellowship of other believers. These front-lines workers were enabled by those doing the faithful work and ministry of *sending*.

Sending Gone Wrong

On the other hand, sadly, front-lines workers can be all but forgotten. "Supporting" churches can either lose communication over time or become irrelevant to the task of mission.

I recently listened to the testimony of one missionary couple who, after several years of faithful missionary service, returned to their home church completely burned out. The immensity of the trials that had befallen them had left them defeated, deflated, and borderline depressed. But unfortunately, relaying their story to an old church friend only took them from bad to worse. In a feeble attempt at empathy, this dear church woman compared this couple's mission field disaster to her own grievances in picking out colors for her new home. Though many years have passed since that event, this missionary couple still tells this story as representative of the cold reception to which many missionaries have grown accustomed at even their home churches.

The Effective Sender

The key to a successful sending ministry is not so much understanding and empathizing with the missionary. More than likely, this would be next to impossible anyway with the highly varied and unusual personality changes, experiences, and spirituality that missionaries often develop in foreign lands.

However, what each sender *can* be is actively and intentionally supportive and encouraging. Many individuals and churches are faithful check writers but not necessarily faithful prayers and communicators. The friendly exchange of letters, emails, updates, and prayers will convey worth and importance. Conversely, the lack of validating communication can be one of the toughest discouragements, especially in beginning a new missionary journey.

The other essential task of the sender is as a promoter of missions, especially in churches with weak or even no missions emphasis. For example, only a fraction of one per cent of church giving is actually directed toward missions. An effective advocate for missions can help stir up a passion among God's people that will propel them toward a deeper and fuller understanding of the Church's role in Kingdom expansion.

The Power of Together

In the end, our roles in the mission of God will be as varied as the people who fill them. No two people are the same, so even people with similar gifts and callings can express their ministry in very different ways. This is the beauty of the body of Christ, that each of us, though called as bold gospel witnesses, each have a distinct, purposeful, and powerful role to play in working together to spread the aroma of Christ both here and amongst the nations.

DISCUSSION QUESTIONS

- How would you define a missionary? Is everyone a missionary?

- What are some characteristics of a missionary call?

- Describe some of the basic reasons that missionaries fail and how to avoid it?

- Why is the role of sender important and what are some of the ways a sender can be effective?

DOING MISSIONS

*"Some wish to live within the sound of
a chapel bell; I wish to run a rescue shop
within a yard of hell."*
– C. T. Studd

Short-term Missions

It has been estimated that between one and four million Americans take short-term mission trips every year spending hundreds of millions if not billions of dollars. That's closely representative of the population and GDP of small countries. In other words, the amount of money just Americans spend on short-term missions is equivalent to the incomes of entire nations.

And while that figure continues to increase, the number of long-term missionaries is declining. Apparently, short-term trips do not translate into long-term commitments. But besides the prospect for long-term missions, what is the value of short-term missions? Let's explore.

An Unlikely Pair

My wife and I are an unlikely pair, to say the least. I grew up in the lap of luxury in an upper-class American home over five times the size of the average home of the day. I had every amenity and opportunity at my disposal and lived in want for nothing.

Vio, my wife, was born into the poorest country in Europe where she lived with her family in a small subsistence farming village in the Communist bloc of Eastern Europe. Most of her possessions were donated, and most of her childhood was spent with a hoe in hand farming the fields surrounding her home. At eleven years old, Vio received her first Christmas gift, a shoebox full of little toys and candies from the Western world, much as the ones I had mindlessly packed and sent out of my abundance as a wealthy American boy.

In my younger years, I was extremely naïve to the needs around me, especially anything outside of America. My idea of missions and generosity amounted to little more than packing all my excess toys, candies, and second-hand clothes into plastic bags so that some Santa Claus adventurer could take them to people about whom I knew and cared little to nothing. My greatest concern in giving my old items away was that they be replaced by new ones, and if I could be regarded as "generous" in the process, well that was all the better, especially for my conscience.

Eventually, that would all change and particularly now that my wife and I have been married for quite some time. We still pack the same shoeboxes together at Christmas time, but now I do so purposefully and prayerfully—and with the knowledge that those shoeboxes (and my efforts) are just a small spindle in the wheel of gospel ministry.

But more than change the way I packed shoeboxes, my cross-cultural marriage invited me into a different world. I now had two very different homes halfway across the world from one another, and I was struggling to fill the gap in between.

My ethnocentristic instincts told me that my new second home just needed more Western solutions, and that those solutions would be best packaged in the form of short-term mission trips. My naivety glistened like a sour apple, pleasing to the eyes but tough to swallow.

At this point in life, I had actually been on numerous short-term mission trips to a long list of countries, more than I'd care to admit. But never had I experienced what it was like for a team to come knocking at *my* village door. Even the teams I had hosted as a more long-term missionary in Asia had not prepared me for the roller coaster ride of actually seeing and experiencing missions from the inside out.

A Case Study for Short-term Missions

My wife's family and I had connected with a church from Western Europe and invited them to our little village to do ministry. We weren't exactly sure what that would look like, but that's nothing new for many of these short-term trips.

The day finally arrived when we would greet our little angels at the local train station where a whopping seventy-two of them stepped off the coaches, one third of whom would be stopping in for dinner at our place.

We ended up having to rent a bus just to get the group to the village and were just in time for dinner only to find out that our mission heroes required meat with their meals. Of course, we obliged since, after all, the group had sacrificed so much time and money to be with us that week. My mother-in-law, along with some of the other village women, went to work slaughtering the chickens in their gardens.

After dinner, we sat down to map out a plan for the week, but the team had trimmed our previously agreed work budget of $2,000 to a mere $500 due to an unexpected shortage of finances at their home church. This was notwithstanding the thousands they had budgeted for their travel expenses. Unfortunately, we had already furnished many of the materials for the projects from our own pockets, and the remaining materials, unbeknownst to the rest of us, would be financed through my brother-in-law to save our family's "face" in the village.

Communication was also an immediate problem in having to translate from the missionaries' first language to English and finally into the local language because there wasn't anyone who knew both the missionaries' first language and the local language.

To make matters even more interesting, the church in the village was extremely traditional, while our missionaries were from a fairly charismatic background. For starters, we listened to a female pastor address the church in a tradition where only men are allowed to preach and with a sermon that was largely, and perhaps even intentionally, lost in translation. Later on in the week, the missionaries offered to take the local youth on a camping trip. Many of them came back theologically confused when they were introduced to new charismatic ideas and techniques. Some were even baptized, unbeknownst to their families or the local pastor. The mission team came back from the outing charged and enthused, while the rest of us grimaced with the work of addressing foreign theology. We also grieved the loss of celebrating a very special community rite of passage of baptism into the church body (which was the work of the local pastor anyway).

We also fought with some of the local hosts over room and board for our missionaries since their toll on local resources was much greater than any of us had anticipated.

In the end, after an exhausting week, everyone was glad to see the team leave, and I wondered how we were all the better for having had them there. Truth be told, in many ways, we seemed even worse off than we started. The local pastor, who was also a full-time farmer, would be left to pick up many of the pieces, and any hope of the group returning was slim to none, that is, if the local villagers had any say in it. Now, that's not to say that there weren't some noble tasks accomplished that week, but the chaos and demand of hosting was simply not worth any benefit we might have received. My experience as a drive-by missions victim had left quite an indelible mark.

Missions Takeaways

Although our experience hosting a short-term team was somewhat less than ideal, to say the least, let's not be guilty of throwing the baby out with the bath. There is a place for short-term trips and certainly for missions in the church. We just need to apply the right wisdom, strategy, and biblical principles to the task. Here are some takeaways toward that end.

1. *Make a Plan.* Ensure there is a clear purpose and objective for the trip. What kind of ministry will you be doing, for how long, and where? Who is your target audience, and how will you reach them? How much will the trip cost, and how can you be a good steward of finances? How will funds be raised, and how will participants prepare? There are endless questions that need to be answered well in advance of the trip.

2. *Train and Educate Participants.* Don't leave home without a basic understanding of what missions is and how to do it well. Study the Bible, learn from others' successes and failures, invite a seasoned missionary to offer some advice—

these are all great ways to prepare. Perhaps there is a source of study such as this book to act as a study aid. And be sure to set standards for participants. Missions is not an activity for unbelievers, but you also don't necessarily need twenty-year long-term veterans either. Use sound judgment in choosing participants and then don't be afraid to challenge them.

3. *Bring skill and talent.* One of the requests I always hear from long-term missionaries is for better skilled and educated short-term helpers. This can also help center the focus of a trip. Are you teaching? Bring teachers. Are you healing? Bring medical personnel. Are you doing pastoral or theological training? Bring ministers and professors. Are you counseling? Bring counselors. Are you building? Bring construction workers. I could go on, but the point is simply to offer those services that we know and not those that we don't. Just having an extra warm body around isn't always a great stewardship decision.

4. *Don't make missions about the sending church.* Using a short-

term trip simply as a teaching tool is begging for trouble, and unfortunately, it is trouble you may never see or realize. That's because those poor little villagers that you "helped" will be the ones picking up the pieces. It's easy to steamroll your hosts when you have a lot of especially young, inexperienced, and (please, no!) even unbelieving participants. While, no doubt, participants will learn a great deal, this is not a healthy focus. Only admit trained, qualified, and mature believers. Missions is not for the faint of heart, and as we already know, takes special God-given gifts and callings.

5. *Respect cultural boundaries.* Do your homework before coming. Is there a local body of believers who have specific customs and traditions? Even if you think your theology is better, don't play hardball with the local church in an attempt to free them from what you interpret to be theological chains. Your message and your service will be much better received if you allow the host church or long-term missionary to be at

the forefront of all that happens. If you cannot work through a local church or missionary, try to find a "person of peace" or point person who can act as a liaison for continuing the relationship and offer access to the people you are serving.

6. *Don't be a burden.* Ease the load. Be gracious to your hosts and avoid being a strain on especially long-term missionaries there who have done the long, hard work of building relationships and finding inroads into the community. You could potentially do more damage in a week than the good that your long-term host has done all year. An attitude of assistance and humility is wonderful to have and will go a long way in smoothing out any of the inevitable areas of tension that you may encounter. Work with what is available. Eat what is provided. Adopt local standards of dress and living if need be. And while it's a great strategy to involve the community in all that is said and done, don't be a financial burden, especially where funds are already tight. This

may take special attention since hospitality is more of a sacred duty in non-Western countries. It is not uncommon for families to put their kids to bed hungry (or worse) in order to feed a large Western belly. Be aware!

7. *Missions is both evangelism and social ministry.* Don't fall off on one side of the horse. When the gospel goes forth, it goes forth in word and deed. If our ministry is in deed only, then no one actually gets saved. Besides, there are plenty of Hollywood celebrities and secular organizations already involved in social welfare. On the other hand, if our ministry is in word only, then we are not practicing what we preach. Jesus healed and provided as he proclaimed the good news. Addressing physical and emotional needs are an expression of our love and a testimony to the validity of our message.

8. *Avoid handouts.* We may find ourselves distributing food or shelter to people such as refugees, for example, who are in need of immediate relief. But for the most part, we ought to be partnering

with a local body of believers or a long-term missionary to minister in such a way that empowers and equips locals to do the work of ministry themselves. They will be there long after you are gone, and you don't want to create a dependency in which ministry hinges only upon your presence or expertise.

9. *Don't neglect discipleship.* Oftentimes we rush in somewhere, save as many as we can, and then rush back home. Sometimes our glowing report of salvations and baptisms is more important than truly fulfilling the Great Commission in making real disciples. Chances are, unless you are ministering in a Western country, most of your "salvations" are simply the product of a culture of hospitality in which the local people feel obligated to please you. In these cultures, if salvations is what you want, then salvations is what you shall get (or anything else for that matter). Don't leave without making a plan for continued discipleship.

10. *Be long-term focused.* Don't plan a mission trip as a "hit-and-run"

experience. Is there a people or relationship that has long-term potential? Maybe your church already has a long-term missionary on the ground somewhere. Think of ways to build short-term trips into lasting relationships and lasting ministries. It's not so much about what happens over the brief course of time that you're actually on that foreign soil. It's about an enduring legacy of fruit that will continue long after you are gone.

Your Mission

Jim Elliot was one of five missionary men martyred by the Waodani people of Ecuador in 1956. He died at the age of only twenty-eight, but with a powerfully enduring testimony to the world, especially in the fiery vigor of his journals left behind. He penned these words on September 24, 1950, as one of his maxims. "Wherever you are, be all there. Live to the hilt whatever situation you believe to be the will of God."

Whatever your station in life, whatever the expression and manifestation of your ministry, you are part of God's collective tapestry of gospel witnesses. Stay the course and, for Jesus' sake, fulfill the will of God in your life until that day when, battered and blistered, you wash up on the shores of Glory where Perfect Love will be waiting for you and for those with whom you shared it—to enjoy forever.

DISCUSSION QUESTIONS

- What are some pitfalls to avoid in short-term missions?

- How do you feel about investing so much money in short-term missions? What are the pros and cons of this investment? What are some alternatives?

- What are some ways that short-term missions can be beneficial? How do we measure the fruit or "success" of a short-term trip?

- How can you personally have an impact in missions? What role might you play?

While uncomplicated enough that you can read it in one evening, you will still be challenged by Aaron's book. Through personal stories, the first half of the book shares the author's encounter with and passion for the call to missions. In the second half of the book you will be introduced to many of the missions issues today such as "from everywhere to everywhere," "the new sending nations of the South and East," and "incarnational missions". The book may just cause you to ask the question, "How does God want me to be involved in the Great Commission?"

Paul Kooistra, Coordinator – Mission to the World (PCA)

Water the Earth: A Student's Guide to Missions is a compelling primer of the mission of God. It gets to the point of God's mission and where believers fit into that mission. Little writes with a clarity and "cut to the chase" style that younger readers will engage with. What is mission? What does the Bible say? What does history teach us and how is God fulfilling his mission today? I haven't read a better, more concise, incisive guidebook! Teenagers, university student groups, and even adult study groups will benefit from *Water the Earth: A Student's Guide to Missions.* I wonder when it will be available in other languages?

Mike Barnett, PhD
Dean, College of Intercultural Studies, CIU

Aaron Little has written an elegant guide to missions, packing history, theology, and soul-searching repentance into a few short chapters. He creatively and convictingly identifies the obstacles and heart problems which keep us from believing in and acting on the Great Commission. This book engages us to not only obey Christ's call to love the world, but to do so for the right reasons – weaving together the personal, the theological and the practical into an inspiring reminder of our true purpose, to make God known.

Thor Sawin, PhD
Professor, Monterey Institute of International Studies

AUTHOR INFORMATION

Aaron Little has been a missionary on five continents and a student of missions, religion, and global studies at Samford University, Columbia International University (M.Div.), and the U.S. Center for World Mission, notwithstanding his cross-cultural marriage to his wife, Vio.

PURPOSE STATEMENT

With a level of globalism unfathomable to generations before us, every people group on earth is barely an arm's reach away. There are now between one and four million just Americans going on short-term mission trips every year, spending hundreds of millions if not billions of dollars, making this book the essential primer for every student or adult in preparing the way. Take a journey through the Bible, through history, and through the life of a missionary as we unpack just what exactly missions is and how to do it well.

MASTERED BY GRACE

I love backpacking. There's nothing like hiking into a remote destination (especially in the mountains), pitching a tent and enjoying a dinner cooked over an open fire. Even potted meat tastes amazing in the middle of the woods!

If you have ever been camping like this, you know that rain can be a real downer. On one particular trip, several of my friends and I were backpacking in the Appalachian Mountains located along the eastern side of the United States. We were only about two miles in on a ten-mile trip when the skies opened up and it started pouring! Even though the rain only lasted about twenty minutes, I was soaked—especially my boots.

After the rains stopped, my friends stopped and put on dry socks from their backpacks. I didn't. I just wanted to get to the campsite, even though it was still eight miles ahead. I paid for that decision. After about an hour, my feet were burning and I was developing some big blisters. But, I pressed on. I even resisted my friends' offer to stop, playing it off as if it wasn't that bad. I was trying to be a true man who doesn't feel pain!

When we arrived at the campsite that evening, I had blisters all over my feet. Some were bleeding. Because of my pride, my feet were badly hurt and we had to change our hiking schedule for that trip.

GRANTED TO COME

Like my pride in resisting the rest and comfort of my friends' offer to stop, God is resisted until God chooses to overcome the sinner by grace. Those who remain in their sin remain in their stubbornness and resistance. They remain rebels at heart! The reason for this is that the unbeliever—apart from God's overcoming grace—is completely unable to come to God on his or her own (Romans 8:7).

Reformed theology teaches that, when God effectually draws a person to faith in Christ, that person will surely come. Historically, this is called the doctrine of

Irresistible Grace. Before time began God chose a people to be saved. Jesus taught, "All that the Father gives me will come to me, and whoever comes to me I will never cast out" (John 6:37). The Father gives his people to his Son and those people "will come" to him.

Jesus said, "No one can come to me unless the Father who sent me draws him" (John 6:44). The word for "draw" here means more than simple enticing and wooing. For example, in Acts 16:19, Paul and Silas are "dragged" into prison. The same Greek word is used. If the Father "draws" a sinner by grace to Christ, he will surely come by grace to Christ. In the same chapter where Paul and Silas are dragged into prison, a woman named Lydia hears the gospel preached by Paul. Luke writes, "The Lord opened her heart to pay attention to what was said by Paul" (Acts 16:14).

Jesus clarifies this point even further: "No one can come to me unless it is granted him by the Father" (John 6:65). Note Jesus' use of the word "unless." The only way that we can enter into a saving relationship with Jesus is if God the Father "grants" us to come. Apart from this gracious act of God, no one can come to Jesus.

THE SECOND BIRTH

Typically, nothing good happens late at night. That's when thieves break in and steal. That's when evil plots are executed. Under the cover of darkness, all sorts of bad things happen. But, there's always the exception.

One of these exceptions came when a Pharisee and ruler of the Jews named Nicodemus "came to Jesus by night" (John 3:2). He had some questions that he probably felt embarrassed to ask in broad daylight. He didn't want to ruin his reputation in the Jewish community. So this "Nick at Night" shows up during the time of Passover in Jerusalem.

Nicodemus tells Jesus, "Rabbi, we know that you are a teacher come from God, for no one can do these signs that you do" (v. 2). Jesus said to him, "Truly, truly, I say to you, unless one is born again he cannot see the kingdom of God" (v. 3). At this, Nicodemus was confused and didn't understand. He asks, "How can a man be born when he is old? Can he enter a second time into his mother's womb and be born?" (v. 4).

If we were there, we might ask the same thing. How can a person be born again? Jesus' answer is remarkable: "Truly, truly, I say to you, unless one is born of water and the Spirit, he cannot enter the kingdom of God. That which is born of the flesh is flesh, and that which is born of the Spirit is spirit" (v. 5-6). Everyone is born into this world somehow. I'll let you do the research on that! But only those who are "born of the Spirit" can enter the kingdom of God. This second birth—called regeneration—is something that God does.

GOD'S GRACIOUS WILL

You have probably seen a variety of styles of music in churches around where you live. Sometimes, this variety has led to "worship wars" within the church. The battles lines are often drawn between traditional and contemporary, reverent and celebratory. However, biblically-based, gospel-driven, Christ-centered and Reformed songs and hymns are being written all the time. In a recent hymn— "Hymn to a Gracious Sovereign" (2005)— Neil Barham penned these words:

O God the deep immutable,
the changeless, wise and still,
You're the absolute, eternal One;
You wield the sovereign will.
Deep Heav'n itself and even time
must bend beneath your sway.
With a whispered thought you banish
night in a flash of blinding day.

What's interesting about this hymn is the stress upon God's sovereignty. Typically, God's sovereignty is brushed under the rug because it is oftentimes offensive. However, there is an important lesson to learn here.

If a person could resist God's sovereign will, God's will would cease to be sovereign. We've learned already that all things, including our salvation, happen "according to the purpose of [God's] will" (Ephesians 1:5). God's will is that which he desires to do and then put into action. It is desire made effective. Or, to put it another way, it is God's desire and purpose displayed in time and space.

In Romans 9:19, the apostle Paul asks the rhetorical question, "Who can resist his will?" Answer: Nobody. We don't even have the right to raise any objection to

God's sovereign will. God is God and is perfectly free to do that which he pleases. For God's elect, God graciously performs a divine heart transplant, replacing your "heart of stone" (Ezekiel 36:26) with one that loves and desires him. If God calls you by grace, you will surely come by grace.

I'VE CALLED YOU BY NAME!

One of my favorite books is *The Pilgrim's Progress* by John Bunyan. It is one of the best-selling books of all time. It tells the story of Christian and his journey from the City of Destruction to the Celestial City of heaven. Along the way, he encounters all sorts of dangers and violent people. He also meets a few friends. One of these friends is Hopeful.

In a dramatic scene, Christian and Hopeful find themselves crossing a great River (symbolizing death). Christian sees the waves rising up and he begins to doubt whether or not he can make it to the Celestial City. But he remembers God's promise from Isaiah: "Fear not, for I have redeemed you; I have called you by name, you are mine. When you pass through the waters, I will be with you; and through the rivers, they shall not overwhelm you" (Isaiah 43:1-2).

Bunyan then writes, "Christian therefore presently found ground to stand upon, and so it followed that the rest of the river was but shallow; but thus they got over." God calls his people by name. His calling is the solid ground when all other callings in this world are but sinking sand.

If you are called to Jesus by grace, you are justified. If you are justified, then you will be glorified. As Paul writes, "And those whom he predestined he also called, and those whom he called he also justified, and those whom he justified he also glorified" (Romans 8:30). The apostle Peter links God's calling and eternal election together when he writes, "Be all the more diligent to confirm your calling and election" (2 Peter 1:10).

By grace, God calls sinners to come to Jesus. He removes the wet socks and stony hearts and clothes us with Christ, in whom we find eternal rest (cf. Matthew 11:28). He stops me on the trail of life to give me a new life in Jesus. "He makes me lie down in green pastures. He leads me beside still waters.

He restores my soul" (Psalm 23:1-3). May you delight this day in the God who draws you to himself so that the grace that brought you safe thus far, is the grace that will lead you home.

REFLECTION QUESTIONS

- How might the idea that, if God "calls" you by grace, you will surely come to saving faith bring you comfort?

- Were any parts of this chapter difficult to either believe or understand?

- Could the doctrine of God's sovereign election fit with a belief that denies God's actual and providential saving of a person in space and time?

- What are some ways in which you could specifically praise God for his irresistible grace?

REBELS RESCUED

A Student's Guide to Reformed Theology

by Brian Cosby

ISBN: 978-1-84550-980-4

Have you ever had a shopping cart with a broken wheel? You push it around and all it wants to do is run into the sides of the aisle. If you were to let the cart go on its own, it would immediately turn and smash into that case of pickles up ahead! You are like that shopping cart! The bad wheel is your heart. It's always veering off, leading you away from what you were created to be.

You were created for God's love and glory, but instead, your heart pulls you away from Jesus and into something much worse than a case of pickles. Being a rebel at heart means that you do not have the ability to choose God or even to respond to God on your own, because you are spiritually dead; we all are. Reformed theology teaches that, because we are more sinful than we could ever imagine, it can only be God who takes that broken shopping cart wheel (our sinful heart) and replaces it with one that has both the ability and the desire to seek him and to follow him. By faith in Christ, you are no longer set to smash into the aisles of sinful destruction. No, he promises to carry us in his grip of grace.

GOD'S STORY

A STUDENT'S GUIDE TO CHURCH HISTORY

BRIAN COSBY

God's Story
A Student's Guide to Church History
by **Brian Cosby**

ISBN: 978-1-78191-320-8

- Understand God's story and God's storyline
- Understand your own identity
- Understand the present, and avoid past mistakes

The history of the church is God's pre-determined plan. It's his "Plan A." Despite the sin, corruption, and twisted events in the church's past, God has preserved a remnant, his people. Brian Cosby makes the past come alive in order to explain your identity, explain the present, avoid past mistakes, and to reveal God's story.

Brian H. Cosby (Ph.D., Australian College of Theology) is Pastor of Wayside Presbyterian Church (PCA) on Signal Mountain, Tennessee, and is the author of several books including *Rebels Rescued: A Student's Guide to Reformed Theology.*

Christian Focus Publications publishes books for adults and children under its four main imprints: Christian Focus, CF4K, Mentor and Christian Heritage. Our books reflect our conviction that God's Word is reliable and Jesus is the way to know him, and live for ever with him.

Our children's publication list includes a Sunday School curriculum that covers pre-school to early teens, and puzzle and activity books. We also publish personal and family devotional titles, biographies and inspirational stories that children will love.

If you are looking for quality Bible teaching for children then we have an excellent range of Bible stories and age-specific theological books.

From pre-school board books to teenage apologetics, we have it covered!

Find us at our web page: www.christianfocus.com